THE EVERYTHING BOOK

The Everything Book
The Essential Details About The One You Love
By Arielle Ford

Book Formatting by Amit Dey | amitdey2528@gmail.com

ISBN 13: 978-1-989161-78-4
ISBN 10: 1989161782

THE EVERYTHING BOOK

The Essential Details About The One You Love

ARIELLE FORD

Praise for *The Everything Book*

"Thanks to *The Everything Book,* you no longer have to try to remember or guess about what your beloved's favorite words, acts of service, or gifts are. Arielle Ford offers a practical, easy, fill-in-the-blank book for couples—think of it as 'an owner's manual' that you can use regularly to give your mate what is most meaningful to his or her heart."

— Marci Shimoff,
***#1 New York Times* bestselling author,**
Happy for No Reason

"The Everything Book" is pure gold! Arielle reveals the missing link she's gleaned over decades of seeking to crack the love code reveals the "little details" and simple shifts you can make that will bring overflowing heart joy and happiness into your relationship and your life. I can't encourage you enough to buy this fill-in-the-blank gem of book!"

— Claire Zammit, Ph.D.
Founder, FemininePower.com

"Arielle Ford has the most extraordinary of gifts: She distills love's highest wisdom and turns it into simple instructions that fill our hearts and transform our lives. In *The Everything Book,* she's done it again. What's the greatest lesson of love? To truly *see* the person in front of us. Fill in the blanks of this book, and you'll fill in the blanks of your love! Give yourself and your beloved the gift of this book."

— Ken Page, host of the Deeper Dating Podcast,
author of Deeper Dating: How to Drop the Games
of Seduction and Discover the Power of Intimacy

Table of Contents

Introduction

Whether you've been together three months or thirty years (or more!), there is always more to learn about the one you love.

Unless you have a photographic memory, it's hard to remember all the facts as well as the little details that make someone feel special. And, there are always new and exciting facts to learn about each other's wants, needs and desires.

Think of this fill-in-the-blank book as an "owner's manual," a step-by-step guide that will provide you with a lifetime of care on how to keep each other happy and satisfied!

The book is designed so both partners can fill it out and then share it. It's an opportunity to provide your partner with old and most importantly new details on the big and small ways to make you smile!

Arielle Ford

La Jolla, CA

History

Name on birth certificate ______________________

____

Name I go by ______________________

Date of Birth ______________________

Time ______________________

City ______________________

State ______________________

Height ______________________

Weight ______________________

Hair color ______________________

Eye color ______________________

Significant birth events ______________________

____

____

Mother's maiden name ______________________

Father's name ______________________

Sisters & brothers names ______________________

____

____

Nicknames ______________________

____

Name on birth certificate ______________________________

____

Name I go by ______________________________

Date of Birth ______________________________

Time ______________________________

City ______________________________

State ______________________________

Height ______________________________

Weight ______________________________

Hair color ______________________________

Eye color ______________________________

Significant birth events ______________________________

____

____

Mother's maiden name ______________________________

Father's name ______________________________

Sisters & brothers names ______________________________

____

____

Nicknames ______________________________

____

Favorite childhood toys ______________________________

____

Favorite things to do when I was little included ______________________________

____

____

Kindergarten I attended ______________________________

Elementary School ______________________________

Significant childhood events ______________________________

____

____

____

Jr. High School ______________________________

High School ______________________________

Extracurricular Activities ______________________________

____

____

____

____

Sports played ______________________________

____

____

____

____

Favorite childhood toys ______________________________

____

Favorite things to do when I was little included ______________________________

____

____

Kindergarten I attended ______________________________

Elementary School ______________________________

Significant childhood events ______________________________

____

____

____

Jr. High School ______________________________

High School ______________________________

Extracurricular Activities ______________________________

____

____

____

____

Sports played ______________________________

____

____

____

____

Awards ______________________________

____

____

____

____

Prom Date ______________________________

I wore ______________________________

____

____

It was held at ______________________________

____

College ______________________________

____

Favorite subjects in school ______________________________

____

____

____

____

Religious Activities (baptism, bar mitzvah, etc.) ______________________________

____

____

____

____

Awards ____

____

____

____

____

Prom Date ____

I wore ____

____

____

It was held at ____

____

College ____

____

Favorite subjects in school ____

____

____

____

____

Religious Activities (baptism, bar mitzvah, etc.) ____

____

____

____

____

Family & Pets

Today my family consists of:

wife/husband ______________________________

children (and ages) ______________________________

____

____

____

ex's ______________________________

sisters ______________________________

brothers ______________________________

____

parents ______________________________

grandparents ______________________________

aunts & uncles ______________________________

____

____

____

cousins ______________________________

____

____

____

others ______________________________

Today my family consists of:

wife/husband ______________________________

children (and ages) ______________________________

____

____

____

ex's ______________________________

sisters ______________________________

*brothers*______________________________

____

parents ______________________________

grandparents ______________________________

aunts & uncles ______________________________

____

____

____

cousins ______________________________

____

____

____

others ______________________________

I am ______________________________ *close to my family.*

My favorite relative is ______________________________

____

____

because ______________________________

____

____

____

My favorite animal is ______________________________

____

The first pet I ever owned was a ______________________________

____

____

Ideally I would like to have ______________________________ *pets.*

They would include ______________________________

____

____

I would like to have a ______________________________

because ______________________________

____

____

____

____

I am ________________________________ *close to my family.*

My favorite relative is ________________________________

____

____

because ________________________________

____

____

____

My favorite animal is ________________________________

____

The first pet I ever owned was a ________________________________

____

____

Ideally I would like to have ________________________ *pets.*

They would include ________________________________

____

____

I would like to have a ________________________________

because ________________________________

____

____

____

____

Friends

My very best friend is ______________________________

____

____

Some of my other friends are ______________________________

____

____

The friend that is the most like family is ______________________________

____

____

My funniest friend is ______________________________

My smartest friend is ______________________________

My oldest friend that I am still in touch with is ______________________________

My friend that lives farthest away is ______________________________

The qualities that are very important to me in a friend are ______________________________

____

____

____

My friends come to me for ______________________________

____

. . . and that makes me feel ______________________________

____

My very best friend is ______________________________

____

____

Some of my other friends are ______________________________

____

____

The friend that is the most like family is ______________________________

____

____

My funniest friend is ______________________________

My smartest friend is ______________________________

My oldest friend that I am still in touch with is ______________________________

My friend that lives farthest away is ______________________________

The qualities that are very important to me in a friend are ______________________________

____

____

____

My friends come to me for ______________________________

____

. . . and that makes me feel ______________________________

____

I have lost friends because ______________________________

____

____

Things I like to do with my friends are ______________________________

____

____

____

____

Things I like to do with a group of friends are ______________________________

____

____

____

____

____

Of all my childhood friends I have lost contact with, the one I would most like to see again is ______________________________

____

____

. . . because ______________________________

____

____

____

____

I have lost friends because ______________________________

____

____

Things I like to do with my friends are ______________________________

____

____

____

____

Things I like to do with a group of friends are ______________________________

____

____

____

____

____

Of all my childhood friends I have lost contact with, the one I would most like to see again is ______________________________

____

____

. . . because ______________________________

____

____

____

____

Health

I am ______________________________ *healthy.*

My best health habit is ______________________________

The least healthy thing I do is ______________________________

Exercises I enjoy ______________________________

Exercises I dislike ______________________________

I exercise ______________________________ *times a week.*

Vitamins & supplements I take daily ______________________________

I am allergic to ______________________________

. . . my reaction is ______________________________

The health problems I have ______________________________

I am ____ *healthy.*

My best health habit is ____

____

____

The least healthy thing I do is __________________________________

____

____

Exercises I enjoy ____

____

____

Exercises I dislike ____

I exercise ____ *times a week.*

Vitamins & supplements I take daily _____________________________

____

I am allergic to ____

____

. . . my reaction is ____

____

The health problems I have _____________________________________

____

____

The medications I must take ______________________________

____

____

My family has a history of ______________________________

____

____

____

I expect to live to the age of ______________________________

Illnesses I have had ______________________________

____

____

____

____

When I get sick it is usually because of ______________________________

____

____

____

I have been admitted to a hospital ______________________________ *times.*

I was admitted for ______________________________

____

My health insurance carrier is ______________________________

____

____

The medications I must take ______________________________

____

____

My family has a history of ______________________________

____

____

____

I expect to live to the age of ______________________________

Illnesses I have had __________________________________

____

____

____

____

When I get sick it is usually because of ________________________

____

____

____

I have been admitted to a hospital ________________________ *times.*

I was admitted for ______________________________

____

My health insurance carrier is ______________________________

____

____

Care & Maintenance

Morning rituals ______________________________

____

Bedtime rituals ______________________________

____

I require ______________________________ *hours of sleep per night.*

If I don't get that amount this is what happens ______________________________

____

____

I like to sleep on the ______________________________ *side of the bed.*

I need ______________________________ *pillows,*

preferably ______________________________

I like to sleep with the windows ______________________________

. . . and air conditioning/heater ______________________________

The way I like to fall asleep is ______________________________

____

____

The way I like to be awakened is ______________________________

If I wake up in the middle of the night from a nightmare, please ______________________________

____

____

I like to take ______________________________ *showers/baths per day.*

Morning rituals ______________________________

____

Bedtime rituals ______________________________

____

I require ______________________ *hours of sleep per night.*

If I don't get that amount this is what happens ______________________

____

____

I like to sleep on the ______________________ *side of the bed.*

I need ______________________ *pillows,*

preferably ______________________________

I like to sleep with the windows ______________________

... and air conditioning/heater ______________________

The way I like to fall asleep is ______________________

____

____

The way I like to be awakened is ______________________

If I wake up in the middle of the night from a nightmare, please ______________

____

____

I like to take ______________________ *showers/baths per day.*

This is the activity I prefer to do alone ______________________________

____

____

____

____

____

I prefer the following accoutrements with my bathing ______________________________

____

____

____

____

____

My favorite toothpaste is ______________________________

____

____

____

Body parts I most like having massaged are ______________________________

____

____

____

____

____

____

This is the activity I prefer to do alone ______

I prefer the following accoutrements with my bathing ______

My favorite toothpaste is ______

Body parts I most like having massaged are ______

Feeding Requirements

I need to eat ______________________________ *times a day.*

Preferably at the following times ______________________________

____

____

____

If I miss a meal I get ______________________________

My favorite:

breakfast foods are ______________________________

____

lunch foods are ______________________________

____

dinner foods are ______________________________

____

meal of the day is ______________________________

____

desserts are ______________________________

____

alcoholic/non-alcoholic beverages are ______________________________

____

kind of sweets ______________________________

____

I need to eat ________________________________ *times a day.*

Preferably at the following times ________________________________

____

____

____

If I miss a meal I get ________________________________

My favorite:

breakfast foods are ________________________________

____

lunch foods are ________________________________

____

dinner foods are ________________________________

____

meal of the day is ________________________________

____

desserts are ________________________________

____

alcoholic/non-alcoholic beverages are ________________________________

____

kind of sweets ________________________________

____

My favorite:

restaurants are ______________________________

____

____

____

____

fast food places ______________________________

____

____

____

. . . because ______________________________

____

____

____

____

Cooking to me is ______________________________

____

____

____

My specialties include ______________________________

____

____

____

My favorite:

restaurants are ____________________

____

____

____

____

fast food places ____________________

____

____

____

… because ____________________

____

____

____

____

Cooking to me is ____________________

____

____

____

My specialties include ____________________

____

____

____

I hate the following foods ____________________

____

____

____

____

I'm allergic to these foods ____________________

____

____

____

____

I often crave these foods ____________________

____

____

____

____

... especially when ____________________

____

____

____

____

Foods that give me gas ____________________

____

____

I hate the following foods ______________________________

I'm allergic to these foods ______________________________

I often crave these foods ______________________________

. . . especially when ______________________________

Foods that give me gas ______________________________

What Makes Me, Me!

My astrological sign is ____________________

I am typical of my sign because I have these traits ____________________

____

____

I am not typical of my sign because ____________________

____

____

____

The thing that makes me different from most people is ____________________

____

____

____

Something people may not know about me is ____________________

____

____

____

____

Something I would like people to understand about me is ____________________

____

____

____

My astrological sign is ______________________________

I am typical of my sign because I have these traits ______________________________

____

____

I am not typical of my sign because ______________________________

____

____

____

The thing that makes me different from most people is ______________________________

____

____

____

Something people may not know about me is ______________________________

____

____

____

____

Something I would like people to understand about me is ______________________________

____

____

____

My phobias and superstitions are ______________________

____

____

____

____

People and things that scare me ______________________

____

____

____

____

____

People and things that make me laugh ______________________

____

____

____

Something I would never do is ______________________

____

____

____

Something I've always wanted to do is ______________________

____

____

____

My phobias and superstitions are ____________________

____

____

____

____

People and things that scare me ____________________

____

____

____

____

____

People and things that make me laugh ____________________

____

____

____

____

Something I would never do is ____________________

____

____

____

Something I've always wanted to do is ____________________

____

____

The event that has had the most significance in my life was ______________________

____

____

____

____

The person that has had the most significance in my life is/was ______________________

____

____

____

____

The best way to get me to do something I don't want to do is ______________________

____

____

____

____

I was ______________________ *years old when I left home.*

I went to ______________________

____

____

I learned to drive when I was ______________________ *years old.*

I was taught by ______________________

It was a ______________________ *experience.*

Generally I am a ______________________ *driver.*

The event that has had the most significance in my life was ____________________

____

____

____

____

The person that has had the most significance in my life is/was ________________

____

____

____

____

The best way to get me to do something I don't want to do is __________________

____

____

____

____

I was ______________________________ *years old when I left home.*

I went to ____________________________________

____

____

I learned to drive when I was ________________________ *years old.*

I was taught by ________________________________

It was a ______________________________ *experience.*

Generally I am a ______________________________ *driver.*

I consider my traffic record to be ________________________________

When I'm in heavy traffic I generally get ____________________________

When someone else drives I feel very ____________________________

My most precious possession ________________________________

The one thing I've always wanted, but never gotten is ____________________

Tattoos I have and where they are located __________________________

Piercings I have and where they are located _________________________

I have played hookey from work / school / life to _______________________

I consider my traffic record to be ____________________________

When I'm in heavy traffic I generally get ________________________

When someone else drives I feel very __________________________

My most precious possession ____________________________

The one thing I've always wanted, but never gotten is __________________

Tattoos I have and where they are located ________________________

Piercings I have and where they are located _______________________

I have played hookey from work / school / life to ____________________

Social Views

I ________________________________ *believe one person can make a difference.*

I think the most important social issues on the planet today are __________________

If I were in charge, this is what I would do about them __________________

This is what I am doing about them now ________________________________

The charities to which I contribute time and money are __________________

I ______________________________ believe one person can make a difference.

____

____

____

I think the most important social issues on the planet today are ______________

____

____

____

____

If I were in charge, this is what I would do about them ______________

____

____

____

This is what I am doing about them now ______________

____

____

____

The charities to which I contribute time and money are ______________

____

____

____

I think the most significant difference between men and women is ____________________

The transformational/motivational seminars that I have attended are ________________

Service organizations I belong to ____

Professional organizations I belong to include ___________________________________

My thoughts on euthanasia are ____

I think the most significant difference between men and women is ____________________

____

____

____

____

The transformational/motivational seminars that I have attended are ________________

____

____

____

____

Service organizations I belong to ____

____

____

____

____

Professional organizations I belong to include ____________________________________

____

____

____

My thoughts on euthanasia are ____

____

____

____

Things I Think About

If I could have the world my way I would ______________________________

If I had $20 million I would spend it on ______________________________

If I could meet one person, dead or alive, it would be ____________________

. . . because ____

If I could have the world my way I would ______________________________

____

____

____

____

____

If I had $20 million I would spend it on ______________________________

____

____

____

____

____

If I could meet one person, dead or alive, it would be ______________________________

____

____

. . . because ______________________________

____

____

____

____

____

If I were famous, this is what I would want to be famous for ______________________

If I could have any three wishes they would be ______________________

If I were famous, this is what I would want to be famous for ______________________

If I could have any three wishes they would be ______________________

Upsets & Moods

I have a ______________________________ *temper.*

The early warning signs that I am angry include ______________________________

____

____

____

____

The worst possible things to do or say when I am angry are ______________________________

____

____

____

____

Techniques I use to calm myself down ______________________________

____

____

____

____

Things that make me cry ______________________________

____

____

____

____

I have a ______________________________ *temper.*

The early warning signs that I am angry include ______________________________

____

____

____

____

The worst possible things to do or say when I am angry are ______________________________

____

____

____

____

Techniques I use to calm myself down ______________________________

____

____

____

____

Things that make me cry ______________________________

____

____

____

____

The best way to help me when I am:

angry ______________________________

____

sad ______________________________

____

depressed ______________________________

____

moody ______________________________

____

I need to be hugged ______________________________ *times a day.*

Ten things that can get me in a good mood:

1. ______________________________

2. ______________________________

3. ______________________________

4. ______________________________

5. ______________________________

6. ______________________________

7. ______________________________

8. ______________________________

9. ______________________________

10. ______________________________

The best way to help me when I am:

angry ______________________________

____

sad ______________________________

____

depressed ______________________________

____

moody ______________________________

____

I need to be hugged ____________________ *times a day.*

Ten things that can get me in a good mood:

1. ______________________________
2. ______________________________
3. ______________________________
4. ______________________________
5. ______________________________
6. ______________________________
7. ______________________________
8. ______________________________
9. ______________________________
10. ______________________________

Ten things that can get me in a bad mood:

1. ______________________________
2. ______________________________
3. ______________________________
4. ______________________________
5. ______________________________
6. ______________________________
7. ______________________________
8. ______________________________
9. ______________________________
10. ______________________________

Ten things that can get me in a bad mood:

1. ______________________________

2. ______________________________

3. ______________________________

4. ______________________________

5. ______________________________

6. ______________________________

7. ______________________________

8. ______________________________

9. ______________________________

10. ______________________________

Alone Time

These are the things that I enjoy doing when I have time all to myself:

1. ______________________________

____

2. ______________________________

____

3. ______________________________

____

4. ______________________________

____

5. ______________________________

____

6. ______________________________

____

7. ______________________________

____

8. ______________________________

____

9. ______________________________

____

10. ______________________________

____

These are the things that I enjoy doing when I have time all to myself:

1. ____

2. ____

3. ____

4. ____

5. ____

6. ____

7. ____

8. ____

9. ____

10. ____

My Perfect Day

I would wake up at ______________________________

The first thing I would do is ______________________________

____

____

____

Then spend the rest of the day ______________________________

____

____

____

I would like to spend the day with ______________________________

____

____

The last thing I would do before going to bed is ______________________________

____

____

____

I would sleep with ______________________________

… and dream about ______________________________

____

____

____

I would wake up at ______________________________

The first thing I would do is ______________________________

____

____

____

Then spend the rest of the day ______________________________

____

____

____

I would like to spend the day with ______________________________

____

____

The last thing I would do before going to bed is ______________________________

____

____

____

I would sleep with ______________________________

. . . and dream about ______________________________

____

____

____

Saturdays & Sundays

On Saturdays I ______________________________ *have a routine I follow.*

On Saturdays I like to ______________________________

____

____

____

____

____

____

My idea of the perfect Saturday night is ______________________________

____

____

____

On Sundays I ______________________________ *have a routine that I follow.*

____

____

____

On Sundays I like to ______________________________

____

____

____

____

On Saturdays I ________________________________ *have a routine I follow.*

On Saturdays I like to ____

My idea of the perfect Saturday night is ______________________________

On Sundays I ________________________________ *have a routine that I follow.*

On Sundays I like to ____

Career

When I was a child I dreamt of becoming a ______________________________

____

The best job I ever had ____

____

The worst job I ever had ____

____

The job I would never want to do is ___________________________________

____

My major accomplishments include _____________________________________

____

____

____

____

My biggest failure was ____

____

____

Currently I earn my living as ____

____

____

What I love most about it is ____

____

When I was a child I dreamt of becoming a ______________________

____

The best job I ever had ______________________

____

The worst job I ever had ______________________

____

The job I would never want to do is ______________________

____

My major accomplishments include ______________________

____

____

____

____

My biggest failure was ______________________

____

____

Currently I earn my living as ______________________

____

____

What I love most about it is ______________________

____

What frustrates me about it most is ______________________________

The one thing I would like to change most about my situation is ______________________________

If I had it to do all over again I would ______________________________

My dream career is to ______________________________

What frustrates me about it most is ____________________

____

____

____

____

The one thing I would like to change most about my situation is ____________________

____

____

____

____

If I had it to do all over again I would ____________________

____

____

____

____

____

____

____

____

My dream career is to ____________________

____

____

____

Money

I am ______________________________ *with money.*

I grew up in a ______________________________ *home*

and the main lesson I learned about money was ______________________________

____

____

I tend to spend money ______________________________

____

____

My attitude toward money is ______________________________

____

____

____

I currently have the following monetary accounts/ sources ______________________________

____

____

____

I have ______________________________ *credit cards.*

I pay my bills ______________________________

I stick to a budget ______________________________

I balance my checkbook ______________________________

My credit rating is ______________________________

I am ______________________________ with money.

I grew up in a ______________________________ home

and the main lesson I learned about money was ______________________________

____

____

I tend to spend money ______________________________

____

____

My attitude toward money is ______________________________

____

____

____

I currently have the following monetary accounts/ sources ______________________________

____

____

____

I have ______________________________ credit cards.

I pay my bills ______________________________

I stick to a budget ______________________________

I balance my checkbook ______________________________

My credit rating is ______________________________

I______________________________ prefer to handle my own finances.

My outstanding debts include ________________________________

My views on lending money to a friend __________________________

When asked by a transient for money, I usually ______________________

I ________________________________ *know my net worth and it is approximately* ____________________________

I____________________ prefer to handle my own finances.

My outstanding debts include ____________________

My views on lending money to a friend ____________________

When asked by a transient for money, I usually ____________________

I ____________________ *know my net worth and it is approximately* ____________________

Music & Books

Types of music I like ______________________________

____

____

Music that inspires me ______________________________

____

Music I like to dance to ______________________________

____

Music I grew up on ______________________________

____

The song that brings back the most memories ______________________________

____

____

Songs I find myself singing in the shower ______________________________

____

____

My musical abilities consist of ______________________________

____

____

If I could play any instrument it would be ______________________________

. . . because ______________________________

____

Types of music I like ______________________________

____

____

Music that inspires me ______________________________

____

Music I like to dance to ______________________________

____

Music I grew up on ______________________________

____

The song that brings back the most memories ______________________________

____

____

Songs I find myself singing in the shower ______________________________

____

____

My musical abilities consist of ______________________________

____

____

If I could play any instrument it would be ______________________________

. . . because ______________________________

____

The best concert I ever went to was ____________________

Someday I would like to see ____________________

The types of books I like to read are ____________________

The best book I ever read was ____________________

Worst book I ever read was ____________________

... because ____________________

The book that changed me was ____________________

... because ____________________

The best concert I ever went to was ______________________________

____

____

Someday I would like to see ______________________________

____

____

The types of books I like to read are ______________________________

____

____

____

____

The best book I ever read was ______________________________

____

____

Worst book I ever read was ______________________________

. . . because ______________________________

____

____

The book that changed me was ______________________________

____

. . . because ______________________________

____

____

My views on lending books ____

____

____

My favorite:

musicians are ____

____

____

____

soundtrack/CD ____

____

authors are ____

____

____

____

time to read ____

place to read ____

____

book to recommend ____________________________________

____

fairytale ____

____

classic ____

____

My views on lending books ____________________

My favorite:

musicians are ____________________

soundtrack/CD ____________________

authors are ____________________

time to read ____________________

place to read ____________________

book to recommend ____________________

fairytale ____________________

classic ____________________

Movies & Television

Types of movies I like ____________________

____

Please, no ____________________ *movies.*

Funniest movie I ever saw ____________________

____

Scariest movie I ever saw ____________________

____

Worst movie I ever saw ____________________

____

Movies that bring a smile ____________________

____

____

Movies that make me cry ____________________

____

____

If someone were to play me in a movie it would be ____________________

____

. . . because ____________________

____

Types of shows I can't stand ____________________

____

Types of movies I like ______________________________

____

Please, no ______________________________ *movies.*

Funniest movie I ever saw ______________________________

____

Scariest movie I ever saw ______________________________

____

Worst movie I ever saw ______________________________

____

Movies that bring a smile ______________________________

____

____

Movies that make me cry ______________________________

____

____

If someone were to play me in a movie it would be ______________________________

____

…because ______________________________

____

Types of shows I can't stand ______________________________

____

Shows I grew up watching ______________________________

____

____

____

TV character I am most like ______________________________

____

I like to watch TV in the ______________________________ *room.*

I like to eat ______________________________

______________________________ *while I'm watching TV.*

My views on the remote control ______________________________

I ______________________________ *fall asleep with the TV on.*

My favorite:

movies ______________________________

____

____

____

____

____

____

____

____

____

____

Shows I grew up watching ______________________________

____

____

____

TV character I am most like ______________________________

____

I like to watch TV in the ______________________________ *room.*

I like to eat ______________________________

______________________________ *while I'm watching TV.*

My views on the remote control ______________________________

I ______________________________ *fall asleep with the TV on.*

My favorite:

movies ______________________________

____

____

____

____

____

____

____

____

____

____

My favorite:

movie stars ______________________________

____

____

____

____

theater ______________________________

snacks at the theater ______________________________

____

____

____

TV shows ______________________________

____

____

____

morning show ______________________________

____

talk show host ______________________________

____

sit-com ______________________________

____

mini-series was ______________________________

____

My favorite:

movie stars ______________________________

____

____

____

____

theater ______________________________

snacks at the theater ______________________________

____

____

____

TV shows ______________________________

____

____

____

morning show ______________________________

____

talk show host ______________________________

____

sit-com ______________________________

____

mini-series was ______________________________

____

Sports & Games

The activity I'm best at is ______________________________

____

____

____

Games I like to play ______________________________

____

____

____

Sports & activities I don't like ______________________________

____

____

____

My favorite:

sports to participate in ______________________________

____

____

____

sports to watch ______________________________

____

____

____

The activity I'm best at is ____________________________

Games I like to play ____________________________

Sports & activities I don't like ____________________________

My favorite:

sports to participate in ____________________________

sports to watch ____________________________

My favorite:

leisure activities ____

physical activities ____

My favorite:

leisure activities ____

physical activities ____

Shopping

My favorite:

city to shop in ______

______

mall ______

______

stores to shop in ______

______

______

websites ______

______

catalogs ______

______

designers ______

______

colors for clothes ______

______

sleepwear ______

______

fragrances ______

______

My favorite:

*city to shop in*____

____

*mall*____

____

*stores to shop in*______________________________________

____

____

websites ____

____

catalogs ____

____

designers ____

____

colors for clothes _____________________________________

____

sleepwear ____

____

*fragrances*____

____

Fabrics I love ______________________________

____

____

Fabrics I dislike ______________________________

____

I like clothes that are ______________________________

____

My oldest piece of clothing is ______________________________

____

I love it because ______________________________

____

My sizes are:

dress/suit ______________________________

blouse/shirt ______________________________

pants ______________________________

shoe ______________________________

socks/pantyhose ______________________________

underwear ______________________________

bathing suit ______________________________

hat ______________________________

ring ______________________________

Fabrics I love ______________________________

____

____

Fabrics I dislike ______________________________

____

I like clothes that are __________________________

____

My oldest piece of clothing is ______________________

____

I love it because __________________________

____

My sizes are:

dress/suit ______________________________

blouse/shirt ____________________________

pants ________________________________

shoe ________________________________

socks/pantyhose __________________________

underwear ______________________________

bathing suit ____________________________

hat __________________________________

ring _________________________________

Things I Like

My absolute favorite thing in the world is ______________________________

____

____

____

____

My favorite:

color ______________________________

sounds ______________________________

smell ______________________________

gemstones ______________________________

flowers ______________________________

trees ______________________________

collectibles ______________________________

____

car ______________________________

words ______________________________

quote ______________________________

____

____

day of the week ______________________________

season ______________________________

My absolute favorite thing in the world is ________________________

____

____

____

____

My favorite:

color ________________________

sounds ________________________

smell ________________________

gemstones ________________________

flowers ________________________

trees ________________________

collectibles ________________________

____

car ________________________

words ________________________

quote ________________________

____

____

day of the week ________________________

season ________________________

The best way to surprise me:

at work ______________________________

____

____

____

____

when I get home ______________________________

____

____

____

____

on the weekends ______________________________

____

____

____

on my birthday ______________________________

____

____

____

for no reason at all ______________________________

____

____

____

The best way to surprise me:

at work ______________________________

____

____

____

____

when I get home ______________________________

____

____

____

____

on the weekends ______________________________

____

____

____

on my birthday ______________________________

____

____

____

for no reason at all ______________________________

____

____

____

Things I Don't Like

Sounds ______________________________

Smells ______________________________

Words ______________________________

Colors ______________________________

People that do ______________________________

____

____

____

People that say ______________________________

____

____

____

People that ______________________________

____

____

____

Pet peeves ______________________________

____

____

____

____

Sounds ______________________________

Smells ______________________________

Words ______________________________

Colors ______________________________

People that do ______________________________

____

____

____

People that say ______________________________

____

____

____

People that ______________________________

____

____

____

Pet peeves ______________________________

____

____

____

____

Spirituality

As a child, my religious upbringing was ______________________________

____

What I believe about God now is ______________________________

____

____

____

____

My image of God is ______________________________

____

____

____

____

Today my spiritual practice includes ______________________________

____

____

____

____

Daily rituals I practice are ______________________________

____

____

____

As a child, my religious upbringing was ____________________________

What I believe about God now is ____________________________

My image of God is ____________________________

Today my spiritual practice includes ____________________________

Daily rituals I practice are ____________________________

I also believe in ______________________________

____

____

____

____

I plan to raise my children to believe that ______________________________

____

____

____

____

I have ______________________________ *a mystical experience.*

It was ______________________________

____

____

____

____

The spiritual leaders (living or deceased) I would like to meet are ______________________________

____

____

____

I believe that when you die you ______________________________

____

____

I also believe in ____

I plan to raise my children to believe that __________________________

I have ______________________________ *a mystical experience.*

It was ____

The spiritual leaders (living or deceased) I would like to meet are ________________

I believe that when you die you ________________________________

When I die I would like my funeral/memorial to ______________________________

____

____

____

____

____

____

I want to be ________________________ *buried/* __________________ *cremated*

. . . when I die, and have my remains ______________________________

____

____

____

I am ____ *organ donor.*

I have ____ *made a last will and testament*

. . . and you can find a copy of it ______________________________

____

____

____

My epitaph will read ____

____

____

____

____

When I die I would like my funeral/memorial to ______________________

____

____

____

____

____

____

I want to be ______________ *buried/* ______________ *cremated*

. . . when I die, and have my remains ______________________

____

____

____

I am ______________________ *organ donor.*

I have ______________________ *made a last will and testament*

. . . and you can find a copy of it ______________________

____

____

____

My epitaph will read ______________________

____

____

____

____

Dating

I ____ *to be spontaneous.*

The first thing that attracts me to someone is ____________________________

The qualities I look for are ____

My idea of a great date is ____

Other ideas for dates I would enjoy are ______________________________

I ____ to be spontaneous.

The first thing that attracts me to someone is ______________________________

____

____

____

The qualities I look for are ____

____

____

____

My idea of a great date is ____

____

____

____

____

____

Other ideas for dates I would enjoy are _________________________________

____

____

____

____

____

Unusual dates I'd love to go on: ____________________

The kinds of dancing I like are ____________________

My views on blind dates are ____________________

Things I would not enjoy doing on a date are ____________________

Unusual dates I'd love to go on: ____

The kinds of dancing I like are ____

My views on blind dates are ____

Things I would not enjoy doing on a date are __________________________________

Romance

I consider myself to be ______________________________ *romantic.*

Romance is a ______________________________ *priority in my life.*

My favorite time of day for romance is ______________________________

____

My idea of a romantic encounter is ______________________________

____

____

____

____

____

One of my fantasies for a romantic night is to ______________________________

____

____

____

____

I think the most romantic place in the world is ______________________________

____

____

The music that puts me in a romantic mood is ______________________________

____

____

I consider myself to be ______________________________ romantic.

Romance is a ______________________________ priority in my life.

My favorite time of day for romance is ______________________________

____

My idea of a romantic encounter is ______________________________

____

____

____

____

____

One of my fantasies for a romantic night is to ______________________________

____

____

____

____

I think the most romantic place in the world is ______________________________

____

____

The music that puts me in a romantic mood is ______________________________

____

____

The movies that put me in a romantic mood are ______________________

____

____

____

____

The following things put a damper on romance ______________________

____

____

____

____

My idea of a very romantic gift is ______________________

____

____

____

____

The least romantic gift I every received from anyone is ______________________

____

____

____

The most romantic thing anyone has ever done for me was ______________________

____

____

____

The movies that put me in a romantic mood are ______________________________

____

____

____

____

The following things put a damper on romance ______________________________

____

____

____

____

My idea of a very romantic gift is ______________________________________

____

____

____

____

The least romantic gift I every received from anyone is ____________________

____

____

____

The most romantic thing anyone has ever done for me was ___________________

____

____

____

When I ask for romance, what I really want is ______________________________

____

____

____

____

____

____

____

The most significant romantic relationships in my life have been ________________

____

____

____

____

____

____

____

What really worked in my relationships in the past was ______________________

____

____

____

____

____

____

When I ask for romance, what I really want is ______________________________

The most significant romantic relationships in my life have been ______________________________

What really worked in my relationships in the past was ______________________________

The former lover I would like to know better is ______________________________

____

because ____

____

____

____

The fairytale, which has most influenced my thinking about romance, was __________

____

____

because ____

____

____

____

The songs and movies, which have most influenced my thinking about romance were ____

____

____

____

If a romantic relationship needed help, I would ________________ *be willing to go to a couples counselor .*

My position on monogamy is ____

____

____

____

The former lover I would like to know better is ______________________________

____

because ____

____

____

____

The fairytale, which has most influenced my thinking about romance, was ____________

____

____

because ____

____

____

____

The songs and movies, which have most influenced my thinking about romance were ____

____

____

____

If a romantic relationship needed help, I would __________________ *be willing to go to a couples counselor.*

My position on monogamy is ____

____

____

____

Relationships

I ______________________________ *being in a committed relationship.*

Most of my friends are ______________________________

in a committed relationship.

My role models for relationships are ______________________________

____

____

____

The woman who most influenced me in the area of a relationship was __________

____

____

The man who has most influenced me was ______________________________

____

____

The longest platonic relationship I have had is ______________________________

____

____

The longest romantic relationship I have had is ______________________________

The recurring complaints I've had about relationships (romantic or platonic) that I've been in is ______________________________

____

____

____

I ______________________________ being in a committed relationship.

Most of my friends are ______________________________

in a committed relationship.

My role models for relationships are ______________________________

____

____

____

The woman who most influenced me in the area of a relationship was ____________

____

____

The man who has most influenced me was ______________________________

____

____

The longest platonic relationship I have had is ______________________________

____

____

The longest romantic relationship I have had is ______________________________

The recurring complaints I've had about relationships (romantic or platonic) that I've been in is ______________________________

____

____

____

The recurring praises I've had about relationships (romantic or platonic) ______________

____

____

____

____

The lessons(s) I have learned from relationships ______________

____

____

____

____

The lessons(s) I still have to learn from relationships ______________

____

____

____

____

My parents are/were married for ______________ *years.*

It was a ______________ *marriage.*

How it affected me ______________

____

____

____

____

____

The recurring praises I've had about relationships (romantic or platonic) ____________

____

____

____

____

The lessons(s) I have learned from relationships ____________________

____

____

____

____

The lessons(s) I still have to learn from relationships ____________________

____

____

____

____

My parents are/were married for ______________________ *years.*

It was a ______________________ *marriage.*

How it affected me ______________________

____

____

____

____

____

I can tolerate just about anything in a relationship except ______________________

____

____

____

____

If I had a crystal ball, I would predict that in five years ______________________

____

____

____

____

I believe that pre-nuptial agreements are ______________________

____

____

____

____

My ideal wedding would be ______________________

____

____

____

____

____

____

____

I can tolerate just about anything in a relationship except ______________________

____

____

____

____

If I had a crystal ball, I would predict that in five years ______________________

____

____

____

____

I believe that pre-nuptial agreements are ______________________

____

____

____

____

My ideal wedding would be ______________________

____

____

____

____

____

____

____

Sex

I was ______________________________ *years old the first time I had sex.*

The best part about it was ______________________________

____

The worst part was ______________________________

____

I think the three sexiest men on the planet today are ______________________________

____

____

____

I think the three sexiest women on the planet today are ______________________________

____

____

Someone I've always wanted to make love with is ______________________________

____

____

The best sexual escapade I ever had was ______________________________

____

____

The worst was ______________________________

____

____

I was ______________________ years old the first time I had sex.

The best part about it was ______________________

____

The worst part was ______________________

____

I think the three sexiest men on the planet today are ______________________

____

____

____

I think the three sexiest women on the planet today are ______________________

____

____

Someone I've always wanted to make love with is ______________________

____

____

The best sexual escapade I ever had was ______________________

____

____

The worst was ______________________

____

____

Favorite positions ______________________________

____

____

Least favorite ______________________________

____

Favorite locations ______________________________

____

____

Least favorite ______________________________

____

Favorite time of day to make love ______________________________

Least favorite ______________________________

____

Favorite lighting ______________________________

____

____

Favorite music ______________________________

____

____

Something I've always wanted to try and haven't is ______________________________

____

____

____

Favorite positions ______________________________

____

____

Least favorite ______________________________

____

Favorite locations ______________________________

____

____

Least favorite ______________________________

____

Favorite time of day to make love ______________________________

Least favorite ______________________________

____

Favorite lighting ______________________________

____

____

Favorite music ______________________________

____

____

Something I've always wanted to try and haven't is ______________________________

____

____

____

Special things I really like ______________________________

____

____

____

Erogenous zones ______________________________

____

____

____

I am most in the mood for sex ______________________________

____

____

Overall, I am ______________________________ *affectionate.*

Public displays of affection make me ______________________________

____

My favorite part of my body is ______________________________

____

The part of my body I most like to have touched is ______________________________

____

Kissing for me is like ______________________________

My ideal partner would like to have sex ______________________________

times a ______________________________

And it could take as long as ______________________________

____

Special things I really like ______________________________

____

____

____

Erogenous zones ______________________________

____

____

____

I am most in the mood for sex ______________________________

____

____

Overall, I am ______________________________ *affectionate.*

Public displays of affection make me ______________________________

____

My favorite part of my body is ______________________________

____

The part of my body I most like to have touched is ______________________________

____

Kissing for me is like ______________________________

My ideal partner would like to have sex ______________________________

times a ______________________________

And it could take as long as ______________________________

____

Sometimes I ______________________________ *a "quickie."*

During sex I am ______________________________

____

____

I would describe my orgasms as ______________________________

____

____

Immediately after orgasm I need you to ______________________________

____

____

After making love I like to ______________________________

____

____

Making love during menstruation ______________________________

____

____

My favorite store to buy oils, lotions and potions is ______________________________

____

____

The type of sex that really turns me off is ______________________________

____

____

____

Sometimes I ______________________________ *a "quickie."*

During sex I am ______________________________

____

____

I would describe my orgasms as ______________________________

____

____

Immediately after orgasm I need you to ______________________________

____

____

After making love I like to ______________________________

____

____

Making love during menstruation ______________________________

____

____

My favorite store to buy oils, lotions and potions is ______________________________

____

____

The type of sex that really turns me off is ______________________________

____

____

____

Sexual Fantasies

I have always wanted to "do it" in the following places ____________________

My top three sexual fantasies include ____________________

I have always wanted to "do it" in the following places ______________________________

____

____

____

____

____

____

____

____

____

My top three sexual fantasies include ______________________________

____

____

____

____

____

____

____

____

____

____

Sex toys I enjoy are ______________________________

____

____

____

____

____

The kinkiest thing I have ever done is ______________________________

____

____

____

____

____

____

I ______________________________ *sex with more than one partner.*

If I knew someone was watching, I would ______________________________

____

____

____

____

____

____

____

I ______________________________ *dirty talk.*

Sex toys I enjoy are ____

____

____

____

____

____

The kinkiest thing I have ever done is ______________________________

____

____

____

____

____

____

I ____ *sex with more than one partner.*

If I knew someone was watching, I would ____________________________

____

____

____

____

____

____

____

I ____ *dirty talk.*

Holidays & Celebrations

My favorite holiday is ______________________________

____

because ______________________________

____

____

How I like to spend:

New Year's Eve ______________________________

____

____

____

____

____

Valentine's Day ______________________________

____

____

____

____

Easter/Passover ______________________________

____

____

____

My favorite holiday is ____

____

because ____

____

____

How I like to spend:

New Year's Eve ____

____

____

____

____

____

Valentine's Day ____

____

____

____

____

Easter/Passover ____

____

____

____

Mother's Day ______________________________

____

____

____

____

Memorial Day weekend ______________________________

____

____

____

____

Father's Day ______________________________

____

____

____

____

Fourth of July ______________________________

____

____

____

Labor Day ______________________________

____

____

____

Mother's Day ______________________________

____

____

____

____

Memorial Day weekend ______________________________

____

____

____

____

Father's Day ______________________________

____

____

____

____

Fourth of July ______________________________

____

____

____

Labor Day ______________________________

____

____

____

Halloween ____________________

Thanksgiving ____________________

Christmas/Hanukkah ____________________

My birthday ____________________

My fantasy birthday celebration consists of ____________________

Halloween ____

____

____

____

____

Thanksgiving ____

____

____

____

____

Christmas/Hanukkah ____

____

____

____

____

My birthday ____

____

____

____

My fantasy birthday celebration consists of ____

____

____

____

Vacations & Travel

Types of vacations I prefer ________________________

My dream vacation would include ________________________

Ways I like to travel ________________________

Places I want to see before I die ________________________

Places I have no desire to visit ________________________

Most memorable childhood vacation ________________________

Types of vacations I prefer ______________________________

____

____

____

My dream vacation would include ______________________________

____

____

____

Ways I like to travel ______________________________

____

____

____

Places I want to see before I die ______________________________

____

____

Places I have no desire to visit ______________________________

____

____

Most memorable childhood vacation ______________________________

____

____

Most memorable vacation as an adult ______________________________

____

____

____

____

____

If I took a long weekend, I would go to ______________________________

____

____

____

____

____

If I took a week or more, I would go to ______________________________

____

____

____

____

I ______________________________ *like to travel alone.*

People I like to travel with are ______________________________

____

____

____

____

Most memorable vacation as an adult ______________________________

____

____

____

____

____

If I took a long weekend, I would go to ______________________________

____

____

____

____

____

If I took a week or more, I would go to ______________________________

____

____

____

____

I ______________________________ *like to travel alone.*

People I like to travel with are ______________________________

____

____

____

____

My Future

The basics I want for my life (marriage, children, etc.) include: ____________________

____

____

____

____

My ideal house would be ____________________________________

____

____

____

____

In five years I expect to be ____________________________________

____

____

____

____

I plan to ____ *working*

as soon as I am ____________________________________ *years old.*

My other ideas for a career include ____________________________

____

____

____

The basics I want for my life (marriage, children, etc.) include: ____________________

____

____

____

____

My ideal house would be ____________________________________

____

____

____

____

In five years I expect to be ________________________________

____

____

____

____

I plan to ____ *working*

as soon as I am ______________________________________ *years old.*

My other ideas for a career include ____________________________

____

____

____

If I had it to do all over again, I would ____

____

____

____

____

____

____

____

____

My bucket list:

____

____

____

____

____

____

____

____

____

____

____

____

____

If I had it to do all over again, I would ____________

My bucket list:

In Case of Emergency

Please contact ______________________________

____

____

home phone ______________________________

mobile phone ______________________________

email address ______________________________

____

Someone in my office to contact ______________________________

____

office phone ______________________________

My doctors are:

medical ______________________________

phone ______________________________

dentist ______________________________

phone ______________________________

chiropractor ______________________________

phone ______________________________

other doctor ______________________________

phone ______________________________

other doctor ______________________________

phone ______________________________

Please contact ____

____

____

home phone ____________________________________

mobile phone ___________________________________

email address ___________________________________

____

Someone in my office to contact _______________________________

____

office phone ____________________________________

My doctors are:

medical _______________________________________

phone _______________________________________

dentist _______________________________________

phone _______________________________________

chiropractor ____________________________________

phone _______________________________________

other doctor ____________________________________

phone _______________________________________

other doctor ____________________________________

phone _______________________________________

Miscellaneous phone numbers:

name ______________________________

phone ______________________________

name ______________________________

phone ______________________________

name ______________________________

phone ______________________________

name ______________________________

phone ______________________________

name ______________________________

phone ______________________________

name ______________________________

phone ______________________________

Miscellaneous phone numbers:

name ______________________________

phone ______________________________

name ______________________________

phone ______________________________

name ______________________________

phone ______________________________

name ______________________________

phone ______________________________

name ______________________________

phone ______________________________

name ______________________________

phone ______________________________

About Arielle Ford

Arielle Ford is a leading personality in the personal growth and contemporary spirituality movement. For the past 30 years she has been living, teaching, and promoting consciousness through all forms of media. She is a celebrated love and relationship expert, author, speaker, and is the co-creator and host of Evolving Wisdom's Art of Love series. Her mission is to help people Find Love, Keep Love and Be Love.

Arielle is a gifted writer and the author of eleven books including the international bestseller, *The Soulmate Secret: Manifest The Love of Your Life With The Law of Attraction* (published in 21 languages and 40 countries).

She has also written many groundbreaking books including *Turn Your Mate Into Your Soulmate: A Practical Guide To Happily Ever After* and *Wabi Sabi Love: The Ancient Art of Finding Perfect Love in Imperfect Relationships, and Turn Your Mate Into Your Soulmate.*

A long-time "Student of Love," Arielle regularly presents workshops around the world including England, Germany, Italy, Mexico, Kuwait, Canada, Romania, Ireland, Austria and Bali as well as personal growth centers such as Omega Institute, Kripalu, The Chopra Center, Esalen, Alternatives in London, AwesomenessFest, Celebrate Your Life, and many other prestigious venues..

Arielle has been called "The Cupid of Consciousness" and "The Fairy Godmother of Love." She lives in La Jolla, CA with her husband/soulmate, Brian Hilliard and their feline friends. www.soulmatesecret.com

Made in the USA
San Bernardino, CA
16 February 2020

64386510R00097